OPENING MY WINDOWS

By William Eric Stevens

William Eric Stevens
Contact the Author at Opening_my_Windows@hotmail.com

Printed in the United States of America
First Printing: June 2010
ISBN 978-0-557-515516-5

For Allie, Mackynzie

You have been the inspiration of my life and shown me the meaning of happiness.

Juliet

This book would not be possible without your support and help.

This book is for you.

Contents

A Note from the Author

I began to write the poems in this book during a time when I was going through a lot of change and soul searching. I was at a point where I was questioning a lot of things about myself and the world around me. Looking at myself, I have to admit that I did not like the person I had become. There were some things that had happened in my life that I was trying to come to terms with. Since I had made it a point from early in my childhood not to share my feelings with others, I found myself unable to trust or communicate with anyone. So, I picked up a pen and started to put my feelings and emotions on paper.

At first, I found it very difficult to write about what I was feeling. But in time I found it easier to explore the thoughts and emotions that I was experiencing. I found that through my writing I was able to put my feelings and even my pain on paper in an organized manner. And then I realized that when I put my efforts and emotions into creating a poem, I felt better in some way.

In time, I let other people read my poetry and then someone who had read my poems told me that my poetry helped them through a difficult time. I found myself humbled and blessed all at the same time. That something that I had created to help myself actually had helped someone else.

Each poem in this book represents a piece of me and the emotions I experienced during a time of self-discovery in my own life. It is my hope that you can apply some of my feelings and written emotions to help you look at your experiences, as you travel the journey of your existence.

Finally, I also want to say thanks to my friends and family for their advice and support in writing this book. I could not have done it without you. Everyone I have ever met and known...be it good or bad...have influenced my life and made me who I am today. So enjoy everyone! You're in here somewhere.

TRUST

Trust, it is so precious
more valuable than gold.
It can be lost or stolen
but never traded or sold.
It can't be given freely
no matter how kind the thought.
And it's not like friendship,
it never can be bought.
For some it seems so worthless,
and for others; King Solomon's mines.
For some it is given in seconds
for others it takes much time.
From me it is rarely given,
to only but a few.
More valuable than a treasure
to those I give it to.

(February 1996)

PRIDE

I have heard many times that pride
always goes before one's fall.
I feel like I have fallen
but my pride still remains.
All I once knew is no longer true
and the person I was is now a stranger.

I no longer live; I simply exist.

My memories have become my dreams
and my dreams have become my reality.
I often think about what I have become
but my pride still remains.
Like a stubborn, defiant king
surveying his crumbling kingdom.

(February 1996)

PATIENCE

For me patience has nothing to do with virtue;
it is a necessary tool for my existence.
As I face the many tall mountains of life,
patience keeps me climbing with a renewed persistence.
There are times when I find myself overwhelmed
and I become physically and mentally spent.
Patience gives me the strength to carry on
every time I feel that my spirit has been rent.
At times I struggle against the stormy seas of my life
and fight against the waves till I am tired and cold.
Patience then appears as a solid rock in the storm
allowing my faith to reach out and take hold.
When I am lost in the deserts of my failure
and my hope is as dry and parched as my lips.
Patience appears as an ever-flowing oasis
where I can replenish my hope for life in sips.

(February 1996)

BROTHERS IN ARMS

I remember the day
when we first met.
Our last moments together
I will never forget.

The good and bad times we shared
as well as our sadness and pride.
Seem to fade much too quickly
when standing over their graves I cried.

Closer than brothers could ever be
until that cold winter's day.
13 flag-draped caskets in the rain
and somewhere in the distance taps played.

I was not there for their last mission
on a chilly evening when they left on a flight.
Their lives ended in a flash
in the sky on a winter's night.

Not a day goes by when I do not miss them
but I am never really alone.
My Brothers in Arms are waiting for me
in a garden of stones.

(February 1996)

THREE IN ONE

In my life, there are three people
who inhabit the body of one.

a Protector
a Diplomat
a Child

The protector is a soldier,
a valiant warrior brave and true.
No matter the foe or battle
he will always come shining through.

The diplomat is a compassionate soul,
he always wears a smile.
Willing to do whatever it takes,
to go the extra mile.

The child is hardly ever seen,
of the three he is often missed.
His purpose is a simple one...
because of him two more exist.

(February 1996)

A SPIRIT CAGED

Step, Step, and then Turn
Step, Step, and then Turn

When the spirit is trapped
the mind is free to soar.
It often leaves this reality
and then heads off to explore.
Time becomes fragmented
each moment becomes an eternity.
Sometimes the silence is deafening
and memories can become torture.
Things that others may take for granted
you wonder if they really ever existed.

As a child I would stare at animals in the zoo
and wonder why they paced back and forth...

Step, Step, and then Turn
Step, Step, and then Turn

Now I know why...
They were not pacing out of boredom
They were pacing out of desperation .

(February 1996)

LONELINESS

Loneliness, she is a spirit,
my companion in times of despair.
She sits beside wherever I am,
and tells me that someone cares.

She is a warm and caring soul
I feel entranced by all of her powers.
She is there with me in my solitude,
and with her I can talk for hours.

With her I escape isolation,
she takes me to a magical land.
Where she walks beside and laughs with me,
and embraces my desperate hand.

When this world forgets that I exist,
she is standing there at my side.
And when there is no one to talk with
in her I can confide.

And as I go to sleep at night
she sings to me in a beautiful tone.
Loneliness holds me close and kisses my brow
and tells me that I am never alone.

(March 1996)

THE PATH THAT HE HAD CHOSEN

The path that He had chosen
was not an easy one.
A mission from a Father
for His only Son.

He had chosen twelve companions
to join Him along the way.
Eleven truly loved Him,
but by one He was betrayed.

When He entered the holy city
He entered as a king.
In lines they stood to see Him
and His glory they did sing.

One night He prayed in a garden
"Father let this pass from me."
He was free to make the choice
that fulfilled the prophecies.

He was ridiculed and beaten
but He never made a stand.
He was led up to Golgotha
as a sacrificial lamb.

His journey lasted several years
and many promises did He fulfill.
From His birth in the town of David
to His death upon a hill.

The path that He had chosen
was not an easy one.
A path that would save the world
travelled by a Son.

(March 1996)

THE CASTLE

A child once built a castle
a place where he could stay.
It was an internal bastion,
where he was safe to play.

He saw a world so full of pain
with no one by his side.
He built a Keep around his heart
so in it he could hide.

He found that in the castle
on himself he could depend.
Walled up in a protected world
that he knew he would defend.

The child and the castle grew;
another wall for every pain.
It had no gates or windows,
so entry could not be gained.

He kept its construction secret
no one else knew that it was built.
To a world he seemed so happy
to hide all the pain and guilt.

As man he found himself all alone,
and then he realized without a doubt...
That the castle he had so finely built
would not let him out.

(March 1996)

MASKS

Few people really know me
because I always wear my masks.
They hide me from the world outside
and complete so many tasks.

One mask is a Defender;
my symbol of great power and strength.
How far will he go to protect his lord?
Almost to any length.

When he fails then Vengeance appears;
a dark night of rage and anger.
He cares not what he must destroy
to remove me from any danger.

Another mask is a Comedian;
his job is to entertain.
To make others laugh and never see
all his master's hidden pain.

Compassion is a benevolent mask;
from him kindness is always shown.
He comforts and talks with those in pain
so they will not feel alone.

All of my masks have served me well
they hide me from everyone else.
But I wonder if there is one more mask
that hides me from myself?

(March 1996)

MY PRAYER

(based on the Beatitudes of Christ, Matthew 5:3-12)

Lord, teach me to be humble
please show me your way.
Grant me the strength and wisdom
to make it through the day.

Forgive for my sins, oh Lord
for which you were nailed to a tree.
I know that I am not worthy,
but make me more like thee.

Lord, teach me to be patient,
and submissive to your will.
Though the world may stand against me
I will trust you still.

Help me to be righteous, Lord
of your glory, let me think.
Whenever I am thirsty, Lord
of your knowledge let me drink.

Lord, teach me to be merciful
with those who do me wrong.
Help me to forgive them, Lord,
and let my love be strong.

Teach me to be pure inside
like freshly fallen snow.
Let my life be a candle for you
so that the world may know.

Lord, let me be a peacemaker,
and not argue or provoke a fight.
Allow me to be your servant, Lord
and show others what is right.

I know that I will suffer, Lord
because I walk your way.
Watch over and protect me, Lord
for in your name I pray.

(March 1996)

THE DREAM

In a dream I saw Christ walk
up a hill called Calvary.
I heard Him scream in terrible pain
as they nailed Him to the tree.

Soldiers cast lots for His garments
for His crown; thorns were used.
Above His head they hung the words
"THIS IS JESUS, KING OF THE JEWS."

A crowd of people mocked Him,
"Come down if you're the one!
You're just Jesus of Nazareth,
a simple Carpenter's son."

My eyes were filled with horror,
when I noticed I was one of them.
Part of the crowd enjoying the pain
of the Man from Bethlehem.

As He hang there suffering,
I heard Him shout a decree.
"Father, forgive them for what they do."
And then He looked at me.

(March 1996)

EQUALITY

Each person is the same inside
no matter their color of skin.
No matter a person's ancestry
or tribe or clan they're kin.

It's too easy to say we are different
because it's so plain to see.
But why can't we live side by side
in understanding and harmony.

Imagine living on a peaceful world
where all could experience equality.
And each person could enjoy the wonder
that is found in diversity.

Change will never come easily
but just think how it could be...
Instead of saying "us" or "them"
if the world could just say "we".

(March 1996)

GRANDPA WES

My Grandpa Wes was a magical man
he always seemed so full of cheer.
And he could do the most wonderful things
like pull quarters from my ears.

His house was distant journey for me
more than three hours away.
In the cotton fields around his house
was a place I loved to play.

The first time I shot a rifle
he caught both me and the gun
Then with a smile on his face he said to me,
"What the heck was that son?"

I used to sit beside him,
and listen to all he had done.
Like the time he wrestled with the dreaded snake
the deadly Rattle-Head-Copper-Moccasin.

When he came to live with us
he brought magic to my life.
He told me of courtin' and sparkin'
and how to tell if a melon was ripe.

His life was not an easy one,
he worked hard for all he had.
But he taught how to joke and laugh
and I never saw him mad.

I had called my mother from far away
when she told me he had passed away.
As I stood there alone it started to rain
the world cried with me that day.

I often regret that I was not there
when he was laid to rest.
But I'll always remember the magical man
who was my Grandpa Wes.

(March 1996)

LESSON IN THE WOODS

While hiking in the woods one day
I had walked for several miles.
I saw so many different types of trees
of all colors shapes and styles.

But I noticed no birds singing
or animals playing on the ground.
I wondered if I was the only living thing
for miles and miles around?

I became tired and decided to rest
and fell asleep on the forest floor.
When I awoke the woods were full of life
where there hadn't been before.

Squirrels and birds played all about me
their voices a symphony of thunder.
A mother deer and her fawn approached me
and stared at me with an innocent wonder.

Then I heard other people approaching
and as soon as I turned my head.
I realized that I was alone again
and all of the woods seemed dead.

I watched two people walk past me
they did not notice that I was there.
Instead all they could talk about
was why the woods seemed so bare.

After they left I sat there and thought
and I decided that I should
Take my time and experience nature
instead of just walking through the woods.

(March 1996)

A FATHER'S POEM

You are a little princess
so perfect in every way.
Just to see your beautiful smile
takes all of my cares away.

I love to hear you laughing
and to see how happy you can be.
No matter what happens in your life
you will always be part of me.

The days that we spent together
were the best I ever had.
Every night I say a prayer of thanks
that I was allowed to be your dad.

You have given me such a special gift,
the most precious that you could give.
For until I first looked into your eyes
I had not yet begun to live.

(March 1996)

THE UNICORN

THE UNICORN

One night I awoke from my dreams
to the sound of distant thunder.
I looked to the sky but I saw only stars,
and my mind began to wonder.
The sound came again but it wasn't thunder,
but the steady rhythm of a something clapping.
The mystery was solved when I heard the nay
of a horse that I knew was laughing.

I climbed out my window and found a path
that led to a field that I knew to exist.
As I walked down the path I was amazed
by the way the ground was shrouded by a mist.
The moon was high in the dark heavens,
and the earth shined with a moon-lit glow.
That exposed the path and surrounding woods
so I knew which way to go.

When I reached the field I climbed a fence,
and then turned and froze in surprise.
For in the distance I saw a beautiful white horse
with a horn between its eyes.
I watched in awe as this beautiful steed
played in the solitude of the night.
When suddenly a strange, cold fog moved in
and the creature disappeared from my sight.

I stood there for several minutes
doubting what my eyes had just seen.
I was a long way from my childhood years
and had outgrown all those silly dreams.

I noticed my breath forming strange new shapes
like miniature clouds in the chilly air.
Then I remembered the one who taught me to dream,
an elegant lady named Amanda Adair.

She was my next-door neighbor,
and her yard was my private playground.
Almost every day of my boyhood life
around her house I could be found.
Amanda opened my world to literature
as she read from books both new and worn.
She filled my young mind with wonder and dreams,
and of creatures called unicorns.
She told me of their magic and purity,
of their horn and how they were rare.
As I stood there alone remembering her stories
my laughter filled the lonely night air.

I decided to turn and retrace my steps
that would lead me back to my bed.
Where I would be safe to sleep once again,
and put the night's events out of my head.

But as I turned to leave I sensed a presence
and in the fog a shape began to form.
Then suddenly I was standing face to face
with a beautiful white Unicorn.
The creature studied me for several minutes
and finally its gaze fell upon my eyes.
I imagine I looked most peculiar standing there,
with my mouth opened in surprise.

Its flesh was rippled with muscles,
and it was graceful from horn to tail.
Its color was spotless and glowing white
that made even the moon look pale.
A silken mane hung down from its neck,
and a long tail fluttered in the wind.
When I looked into its innocent eyes
I could feel that it was free of sin.

The Unicorn lowered its regal head,
until the horn gently touched the ground.
I reached out to touch it then pulled my hand back,
so not to spoil the purity I had found.

The creature raised its head and looked past me
to where it's gaze stopped on the trunk of a tree.
I looked overhead and saw hundreds of apples
hanging ripely on branches above me.

I smiled at the creature as I lifted my arm
it shook its head as if trying to understand.
From a branch I took an apple
and the Unicorn gently took it from my hand.

As the beautiful animal ate, it watched me
and from me no words were said.
I just stood there and stared in amazement
at the magnificent horse with a horn on its head.

The Unicorn rose up on its hind legs,
and the horn was raised high in the air.
The feathering on the legs danced back and forth,
as if to thank me for the time we had shared.
The slowly the fog began to cover its form,
and the Unicorn drifted away from my sight.
I suddenly found myself standing alone once more
in a field by myself at night.

And as I began to walk slowly home,
Amanda Adair's words once again came to me...

"Unicorns are seen by just anyone child,
but by only those who believe."

(March 1996)

MY WISH

I wish the world was a happy place
a place full of love and joy.
Where people all worked for the good of man
rather than worked conquer and destroy.

I wish that we could live in peace
with our fellow man.
Instead of marching off to war
why not sit together trying to understand?

I wish that children would never know
of the words hunger or poverty
Is it possible to work together
to ensure the world's prosperity?

I wish that there were no disease
and no one lived in pain.
No one would suffer needlessly
and no one would die in vain.

(March 1996)

THE PROCESS

I am often amazed by the process
in which these words I write.
I am not able to control when it occurs
it comes to me day and night.

I rarely choose the subject
rather the subject chooses itself.
Sometimes it's an imagined story
and sometimes a feeling I've felt.

When I write I feel no pain;
I feel no joy or rage.
Everything I am works to bring
life to my words on a page.

When I am done I sit in wonder
pondering the words that I see.
I often wonder how these things
could ever come out of me.

When some people read what I write
they tell me that I could.
Make money by writing for other people
but I don't think that I should.

Because the simple poems that I write
come from a place in me that few people know.
And if I were to sell these to someone else
would I be selling my soul?

(March 1996)

NATURE'S ART

I have seen so many works of art
but I have never been able to understand.
Why people put such importance
in a work created by man.

I see the beauty in the woods at sunrise
when I walk with trees overhead.
Where the rising sun turns the web of a spider
into a portrait of exquisite silver thread.

I do enjoy the art made by men
but it never will compare.
To the art and the beauty created by God.
for all the world to share.

If I should ever build my own home,
God's art will hang on my walls.
For every room will have a window
so that His art can be enjoyed by all.

(March 1996)

THE QUEST

THE QUEST

I awoke in a dream one night
outside a place I had once known so well.
It was the castle that I had built around my heart,
so in it my feelings could dwell.
I wondered why I had been allowed to return
was I there on some type of quest?
To find a forgotten treasure
or to begin a personal quest?

Outside the old fortress there was destruction
where once great trees had stood tall.
All around me I could see many years of attempts
to breach the castle's outer walls.
My feet walked on lifeless, scorched earth
as I surveyed the outer defenses
They still stood firm although battered and burned
and to the outside had not relented.
It seemed every piece of the wall had been attacked
so that an entry might be gained.
But the fortress had no gates or windows
and any entrance could not be obtained.
I also saw several tunnels,
another attempt the walls the breach.
But the castle had such deep foundations
that no one could tunnel underneath.
To the outside world it must seem impenetrable
and most would think the walls were built for them.
But the walls were not only built to keep others out
but to also keep someone in.

I began to wonder if I could still get inside
where a powerful force could not make a stand.
So I went and knelt beside a wall,
and touched it gently with my hands.

The wall became warm as I began to speak,
"*Great wall what bravery you have shown.*
You have served the one who built you well,
now please let him go home."
Suddenly a burning heat engulfed my body
the wall and it stones no longer seemed hard.
I was quickly lifted and transported through the rock,
and was gently set down in a yard.

The place was so familiar to me,
it was a yard where I played as a boy.
Where I had learned to use my imagination
instead of relying on all of my toys.
In front of me stood my castle,
which contained an elaborate keep.
Over the entrance were the words I'd once written,
and seeing them again almost made me weep...

EVERYONE WILL SEE A PIECE OF ME,
BUT NO ONE WILL SEE ALL OF ME.

As I traced the words with my fingers
the door beneath opened to my surprise.
From somewhere inside I heard a crying child,
so I quickly went inside.

When I entered the massive fortress,
behind me the door slammed closed.
Slowly the lights began to brighten
and I noticed that had changed my clothes.
I now wore the garments of my ancestors
a white shirt with a plaid and kilt.
At my waist was the sword of a highlander
with a beautiful basket hilt.

Hanging on the walls all around me
were the memories of my life.
Some brought thoughts of honor and pride
and others of sorrow and strife.

I had searched for what seemed like hours,
looking for the child who had cried.
But this castle was a fortified labyrinth
with so many places to hide.
I felt as though there was someone watching me
as I approached they opened every door.
When I walked into an unlit room
there was light where there had not been before.
Soon I began to realize
that I was not the only one in my old home.
I remember the ones I made and who wore masks,
who had cared for me when I felt all alone.

One mask was worn by a comedian,
his job was simply to entertain.
Another wore the mask of compassion,
and he comforted those in pain.
He who wore the mask of my defender,
was a knight and I was his crusade.

Vengeance wore a very dark mask,
and to protect me war he would rage.

But yet there seemed to be one more,
a wearer of a hidden mask.
His job was to protect me from myself,
and I had never seen him at his task.

I heard a horse and rider approaching me,
the steed's hooves met the floor with a boom.
The walls shook as the two came closer,
and I began to feel a chill entering the room.
Before they appeared, I became very scared
beside me there was a door where I could hide.
As I stepped toward it; the door opened for me
and I saw the word "Chapel" as I went inside.

The Chapel's door closed as I entered the room,
a small place dedicated to God.
Facing me was a man with a silver mask
who gave me a silent nod.
As the rider approached, he motioned for silence,
when the rider stopped outside I suddenly froze.
After a few moments he continued on his journey,
and the man before me quietly rose.
He was wearing the mask of compassion,
and his sliver face showed a reflection of mine.
As he approached he humbly bowed his head
and when he spoke his words were so kind.
"*Pardon me for my rudeness,*
my actions to you must seem strange.
But you've been away for a very long time
And many things have changed."

I asked him what had happened,
and about the crying child that I had heard.
"*My son*", he said, "*Please have a seat and rest,
while I try to answer your words.*"

He told me that even though I had left years ago,
a part of me in the castle I had kept.
And all the people I created to protect me
had continued to serve the part that was left.
I learned that the rider in the halls was Vengeance,
had been released when strangers attacked my home.
And because part of me still felt I needed him
for my protection the halls he roamed.
I asked Compassion since I created Vengeance,
would he still serve me yet?
"*He serves only the part that stayed,
so to him even you are a threat.*"

He told me that my quest was far from over,
and that I still had a long way to go.
But there were others who knew I was coming,
and my path they would help me to show.
As I stood to leave I asked him to join my quest,
but he told me that he must stay.
He said, "*Each of us serve you in different ways,
so I must stay here and pray.*"

I left the Chapel and continued on
wondering who or what I might find.
I had walked for only a few minutes,
when someone's laughter filled my mind.
The sound was coming from behind an open door
that was very tall and wide.

When I stepped inside I was in a Banquet Hall,
and I could not believe my eyes.

Someone had prepared a great feast
with food and drink all over the place.
And eating at the table was a peculiar man
whose mask wore a smile on its face.
He spoke as soon as he recognized me,
and he tried to conceal his food.
"*Pardon me sir for starting without you,*
I hope you don't think me as rude."

I shook my head to tell him no
and he graciously led me to a seat.
He made sure that I was comfortable,
and then gave me a plate from which to eat.
As I ate he danced all around the room
reciting some humorous quotes.
I finally told him that I needed information,
and not a comedian full of jokes.
I could tell that I had hurt his feelings
as he dropped his smiling head.
After a moment of silence he looked up at me,
and very humbly he quietly said,

"*A comedian cannot educate his lord,*
his purpose is to entertain.
But if one can solve my riddles,
then maybe the answers he seeks will be gained."
When I gladly accepted his offer
he quickly cleared all the food.
For a moment his mask said nothing
as if somehow trying to change its mood.

When he spoke I listened intently,
digesting every one of his words.
But all of his riddles seemed so vague,
and I could not understand the things I had heard.

*"You created others to help you,
you remember four, but there are actually five.
The fifth you may not be able to see,
but he is always by your side."*

*"His job is not to listen, or to make you laugh.
He was created to serve his master.
He is not a knight or a vengeful soul,
but he always protects you from disaster."*

*"A knight who is your defender,
will give you an important clue.
But you must not be seen by he who rides,
for he wants to destroy you."*

*"You are on an important quest
to find a child that you heard cry.
And you are the only person
from whom he cannot hide."*

*"Every step that you take
brings you closer to the boy.
And when you finally set him free
then true peace you will both enjoy."*

*"But when you finally find the child,
he will think that he is in danger.
Then one will come charging on the horse of death,
and will attack with an unquenchable anger."*

"When that battle does inevitably come
the blows from your aggressor you cannot defend.
But if you call the name of the forgotten mask
for you he will come and defend."

"Now the mask you've forgotten is a powerful one,
but only when you call his name.
Until then he cannot protect you,
for until you ask he is restrained."

When he finished he stood up and said,
"Sire that is all I can say.
And now that you have rested,
you had better be on your way."

I soon continued on my journey,
and found myself entering the massive Keep.
It was the inner-most part of the Castle;
a place that no enemy could breach.

I stumbled as I turned the corner
where blocks of stone littered the hall.
It looked as though a wall had exploded from within,
and there were burn marks on the walls.
A chill of fear ran down my spine,
when a broken seal I found on the floor.
It was the mark that I had once left
when I had closed a protected door.

The door's purpose was used to contain Vengeance,
to be kept isolated in his private home.
But recent events had brought him out,
and now my Castle he roamed.

Again I heard the booming sound
of a horse and rider coming near.
I turned and ran as fast as I could,
so they would not sense my fear.

I had run for several minutes,
when I finally decided to pause.
I was now in the Castle's Armory,
where weapons and armor lined the walls.
I slowly moved thru the great room,
and examined all the tools of war.
Suddenly I saw a figure move to my front,
a knight armed with a heavy claymore.

He wore a brilliant suit of armor,
and I knew he served my family's crest.
Because he wore the falcons of my family's shield
proudly upon his chest.
The knight's helmet was made of silver and gold
decorated by only a Celtic cross.
Its outstretched arms had holes for his eyes,
so the knight's vision would not be lost.

A noble voice came from behind the mask
as he drew the claymore from his belt.
"*Stranger please fill your hand with your sword,*
and prepare to defend yourself."

As he approached I drew my sword,
then I quickly re-sheathed my blade.
To challenge someone as well trained as he
would have been the last mistake I made.
I told him that I had one question

before I fell from a blow of his sword.
"*What good is it to defend a Kingdom,*
if to do so one must kill its lord?"

The knight studied me for only a moment,
and then quickly fell to his knees.
He pleaded, "*Forgive me, you've been gone so long.*
Please, I did not know it was thee."

I asked him to rise and walk with me,
because I had not seen him for many years.
As we walked I could not see his eyes,
but I sensed they were filling with tears.
We had walked for only a few minutes
when he said, "*My lord, I must return to my post.*
But let me tell you something that may help
you find the answers you seek the most."

"The real treasure of this Castle
is hidden to only but a few.
It is guarded by the birds of prey
that your family gave to you."

I soon continued on my journey,
and I felt as if I had walked for miles.
But I hoped that I would soon see the face
that belonged to the crying child.
The hall I was in ended at a door
which felt like it was made from a boulder.
I entered the room as fast as I could
for I knew my journey was over.

But inside there was nothing but kegs of water
and some grains harvested from a field.
I was turning to leave when I saw a wall
where the stones formed my family's shield.
I stared in awe at the huge coat of arms,
its three stone falcons returned my gaze.
I smiled and laughed to myself when I realized
that falcons were birds of prey.

When I touched the wall, it began to move;
it broke in half and slid to the sides.
Before me was a dark hall that led to room
where a young boy was trying to hide.

Quickly I ran as fast as I could
thru the cold, dark hall.
When I entered the room I saw only a fireplace
and a huge mirror that formed a wall.
As I stood there and stared at my reflection,
I heard the gallop of a horse at full speed.
I knew that Vengeance was on his way
to save the child from me.

The remaining riddles of the comedian
I was trying to solve in my head.
My time was quickly running out,
and soon I might be dead.

I still needed to find the crying child,
and the owner of the other mask.
But here I could find no solutions,
and it seemed such an impossible task.

In the large mirror I saw my reflection
and behind it I knew the boy had to be.
Was the mirror before me the forgotten mask,
that protected the child from me?

I knew no quarter would be given
when Vengeance appeared at the far end of the hall.
He was wearing all black armor
and upon his horse he seemed so tall.

From behind the mirror came a scream,
and the horse stepped forward with a jolt.
The mask Vengeance wore was an opaque black,
decorated with only a lightning bolt.
Fear began to fill the room,
and the air became very stale.
I froze in terror when I saw
that the horse he rode was pale.

His blackened eyes turned red as fire
as he entered the darkened hall.
Storm clouds engulfed all behind him
and he charged forward with a battle call.
Down the hall he raced towards me;
he seemed at one with his ride.
His blackened armor looked as cold as ice,
but I could tell it held a fire inside.

Vengeance had captured my attention,
so much I do remember pulling my blade.
But now it was drawn and would have to fight
this powerful force I had made.

With the sword I struck the mirror
its shattering rained a shower of glass shards.
For just a few seconds I saw the child
whose cries I had heard from the yard.

That is when Vengeance arrived in front of me;
on his arrival the room became as dark as night.
How could I possibly defend myself
against someone who had taken my sight?

The storm clouds that followed behind him
hit the room with hurricane's force.
Through the winds, rain and lightning flashes
I saw Vengeance dismount from his horse.

As he approached he swung his sword.
Its blow snapped my blade in two.
In desperation I threw what was left of my sword,
but to his armor no damage did I do.
His blade wasted no time in finding my arm
and the escaping blood on my skin felt warm.
When I tried to use my damaged appendage,
I saw it was badly torn.

Now that I was injured,
he seemed to feed on my fear.
Within minutes I was lying on the floor,
and I felt my end was near.

As Vengeance picked me up; the child yelled, "*catch*"
and I was thrown against a wall.
On impact something in the wall held onto me,
and would not let me fall.

The dark knight stared at me in amazement,
then he quickly turned to face the boy.
I knew as soon as he picked up his sword
that the child he planned to destroy.

I looked at the wall that held onto me,
and suddenly it all became so clear.
It was the castle that had always protected me,
and no matter where I went it was near.

Vengeance was now moving quickly;
for the child I felt a certain sense of doom.
I felt that if I did not act fast
that this great Castle would become a child's tomb.

I yelled at the top of my lungs,
"Castle, you have always been there for me...
Now for the boy and I please send Vengeance away,
and let us both be free."

Suddenly, there was a great rumbling,
and a shaking came up from the ground.
Vengeance stopped just short of the boy,
and nervously looked all around.

The sunlight invaded as it burst thru the walls,
the golden rays threw Vengeance to the floor.
From behind me a strong wind began to blow
as if someone had opened a door.

And even though Vengeance resisted;
his body rose in the air several feet.
With the wind he was quickly carried away,
unable to stop his retreat.

His powerful horse seemed to be changing,
as its pale color began to change tone.
And then the flesh of the animal began to transform
into a surface of fine marble-like stone.

The wind carried both Vengeance and his storm
back to the place where he had been released.
As he entered his home the door reformed,
and the blowing winds suddenly ceased.

I did not know how long I had slept,
when I woke up on the floor.
I tried to move but could only wince in pain
because all of my body felt sore.
The young boy was now beside me
and he was trying no more to hide.
He was tying a bandage on my injured arm
that was wrapped up at my side.

I noticed the room that we were in
somehow seemed more bright.
All around me were newly made windows
that let in the outside world's light.

The child asked me if I could stand,
and then helped me to my feet.
Then with his assistance we made our way
back to the banquet hall to eat.

Along the way I looked at him and realized
that his face was one my mind had once known.
His face was the reflection of the boy I once was
when I built this castle so long ago.

And while we ate he asked me,
"*Are you here to be my friend?*
It does get very lonely here
but it is better than being hurt again."

I told him that I knew of his pain,
and that I had once been hurt too.
And he smiled when I knelt to him and said,
"*I promise to never let anyone hurt you.*"

To seal my promise I gave him a gift;
a small cross that I had worn for years.
And when his small hand took the cross from mine,
from his touch I felt no fear.

After we had eaten and talked he fell asleep,
and I held him in my arms.
He seemed to sleep so peaceful,
as if he felt safe from any harm.
While I held him I began to think
of the reasons for my quest.

I realized the child was the treasure I had sought,
and now I too was ready to rest.
But as I began to fall asleep
over both of us appeared a quilt.
I knew then I had found comfort throughout my life
here in the castle I had built.

I also knew that the child and I were not alone
when on the quilt five masks I saw.
Four were of those I had met on my quest,
and one was made from the stones of a wall.

(April 1996)

THE RIVER OF LIFE

Each life is like an uncharted river
and within its currents one's conscious flows.
As it follows an unknown course downstream
in both knowledge and substance one grows.

No maps or charts can be your guide
around each bend awaits something new.
Along the way there are obstacles
that can only be navigated by you.

Some get scared and try to swim
back upstream to return to the source.
But it's either struggle in vain or continue on
until one's river has run its course.

(May 1996)

THE ROAD

I once found myself driving on
the road of my memories.
It cut a path through my entire life
where events served as the scenery.

As I drove my life passed by
and I wondered who was in control.
Was I steering the car, or just riding along
on this scenic tour of my soul?

I entered an area that had no hills
and was straight as far as I could see.
I noticed that I was surrounded on all sides
by my life's happy memories.

Suddenly the road I was travelling on
became rough as if it was scarred.
A wind foretold of an approaching storm
and the skies became very dark.

I felt both embarrassed and sad
when I saw the painful events of my past.
Feeling like I was bound and helpless
I wondered how long this would last.

The feelings I had once felt came back to me
and I suddenly became very scared.
I tried to force the car to accelerate
in hopes to pull away from there.

Soon all the scenery was behind me
and the sky began to clear.
I wondered if remembering the bad times
would always bring back the pain and fear.

But when I saw my past in the rear view mirror
The words on it told me that no pain was near...

*"Objects that are seen in this mirror
may feel closer than they appear."*

(May 1996)

NUMBNESS

Numbness has replaced my emotions
as the day is replaced by night.
Inside I feel cold and empty
like a candle that has lost its light.

All of the feelings I used to know
have been replaced by a void.
Sometimes I forget what it was like
to experience anger, sadness or joy.

I often feel like I am falling
into an immense and inescapable hole.
I should feel scared but I am not
because fear no longer lives in my soul.

Maybe my emotions will someday return
and for this I hope and pray...
That emotions will replace my numbness
like the night must surrender to the day.

(May 1996)

AFRAID OF THE DARK

I was a child who was afraid of the dark,
because night terrors filled my head.
They were dreams more worse than nightmares
that filled my nights with dread.
I still remember each dream ordeal
but there is one that surpasses them all.
A dram whose recollection still haunts me today
and makes me fell scared and small.
In the dream I was trapped in a great expanse
and all around me the world was black.
I would try to move but was held in place
by the wind's cold hand on my back.
I felt so scared and all alone
out of fear I would begin to cry.
And then the rain would fall on me
like arrows that were shot from the sky.
The darkness and the wind would not let me move
so much that it seemed hard to breathe.
All I could do was huddle and pray
that it would soon be time to leave.
After what seemed an eternity
I would finally awake to the light
that was always on in my room
so I could sleep better at night.
My family always thought the light was on
to protect me from things I could not see.
But the light stayed on to show me the way home,
from the darkness that held on to me.

(May 1996)

SANDSTORM

It is a raging, non-liquid Tsunami
that crosses the desert like an ocean's wave.
A living creature of sand kept alive by winds
that seeks to capture all in its way.

It has a heart that is made of chaos
that brings control to a sun baked land.
As it travels it zealously attempts to remove
all the objects that have been left by man.

And like and ancient warrior of the desert;
all foes are vanquished with a sweep of its hand
For it attacks and leaves all signs of our invasion
buried under mountains of sand.

(June 1996)

I WASN'T THERE

I wasn't there on the night
when Christ came into the earth.
I never heard the angels sing
to tell the world of His glorious birth.
I wasn't there when He was tested
in the desert for forty days.
When He withstood all of the temptations
and was not led astray.
I wasn't there when He healed the sick,
cured the blind or raised the dead.
I was not one of the thousands that ate
from two fishes and five loaves of bread.
I wasn't there when He was betrayed
in a garden by one of His own.
I did not see the look in His eyes when
another denied Him at the High Priest's home.
I wasn't there when He carried a cross
up a hill known as Calvary
And I did not see the heavens turn dark
as He died between two thieves.
I wasn't there when He came out of the tomb
and conquered both death and the grave.
My eyes did not see Him ascend into the sky
so that He could prepare for us a way.
I wasn't there for one moment that He lived as a man,
but as I look back on my own life I see...
That no matter where I was when I needed Him,
Christ was always there for me.

(August 1996)

MY FRIEND IN THE FOREST

I do not know how long he has lived
in the secluded woods near my home.
But his towering size and enormous width,
can only hint at the seasons he has known.

Every time that I journey to see him;
he greets me with arms open wide.
And he introduces me to all of his woodland friends,
who run around us as I sit at his side.

I talk with him while I lay at his feet,
where the moss feels as soft as felt.
Then I listen as he sings a song with the wind
that is as ancient as time itself.

He stands in a meadow where a house once stood,
but has long since faded away.
Yet he still carries the marks of an old rope swing
where a child spent countless hours at play.

Our relationship exists because it knows no rules,
it is a friendship between a man and a tree.
And because we spend all our time together
just enjoying each other's company.

(August 1996)

I STILL REMEMBER YOU

I am not sure you remember me
but I still remember you.
I am the child that you invaded
and left embarrassed and confused.

No one deserves what you did to me
you took my innocence along with my pride.
And you forced me to grow up much too soon
with a child trapped deep inside.

Did you enjoy the power that came
from the control of a little child?
Was I the only one that you hurt
or were there others that you defiled?

I have often wondered to myself
which of your needs did I fulfill?
And was that need important enough
to use a child for a personal thrill?

(September 1996)

A VICTIM NO LONGER

They use many terms to describe what happened
when as a child you were molested or abused.
But in all cases they tell you that you are a victim
because by someone else you were hurt and used.

You were told to live as if it never occurred
but that proved to be too difficult.
How could you continue to live the life of a child
when your innocence was taken by an adult?

Trust is something that you no longer have;
with it, you put your emotions up on a shelf.
You place barriers between you and everyone else,
because only you can protect yourself.

You convinced yourself to hide all the pain
and all of the memories from your heart.
But there will come a day when you remember it all
and you will feel like your world is falling apart.

The biggest obstacle that you will ever cross
is to allow yourself to trust others again.
You must find the courage to let go and then confide
and convince yourself in someone else to depend.

With the help and support from those who care,
your inner beauty will again be revealed.
You will see that your physical and emotional scars
are actually old wounds that have healed.

Your journey will not always be easy or fun
but each tear that you shed brings a discovery.
Just take your time and enjoy each wonder you find,
on the long path of your recovery.

In time you can finally look at yourself and know
that what happened has actually made you stronger.
And when you can call yourself a survivor
then you will be a victim no longer.

(October 1996)
William Stevens
~a Survivor~

AS I WALK THROUGH FIELDS OF GREEN

As I walk through fields of green
that blow like waves by winds unseen.
Where high above a bird majestically sings
as it sails along on feathered wings.
In the shade I sit beneath some evergreens
and smell the scent of an eternal spring.
I find myself in awe of the beauty in nature's things
and with each new step another wonder it brings.
My soul becomes one with this beautiful scene
as I walk through fields of green.

(December 1997)

ORION

For centuries man has watched you appear
in the night sky above the dark horizon.
An eternal traveler of the heavens
you are the constellation, Orion.

The Greeks chose a mythical hunter
to describe your celestial form.
In Arabic you are known as the giant
to sailors the bringer of storms.

No other constellation looks more like a man
with a body made of stars and space.
Betelgeuse protects your right shoulder
and a nebula hangs from your waist.

(August 1998)

FOR THE FLEDGLING

You often remind me of a small fledgling
who is ready but still afraid to fly.
So instead of soaring you spend your days
staring out at the big open sky.

Each day you hear the wind call your name
to sail with her through clouds of white.
And each night you spend your dreams in the air
gliding along the warm beams of light.

You were born with a gift that few others have;
the ability to shed the earth and soar.
And if tried you might climb the heavens
higher than anyone has gone before.

I hope I find myself near your nest
on the day you decide to fly.
When I will watch you spread your beautiful wings
and then eagerly embrace the sky.

(September 1998)

COLORBLIND

All of my life I have been colorblind,
the inability to see most colors or shades.
So to me most tones are a mystery
and I live in a world of grays.

I feel colors better than I see them,
like the brightness and purity of white.
I have been warmed by the color yellow,
and wrapped in the dark of the night.

The colors I see are quite different
than how they appear to you.
And I do not think about what I cannot see;
I cannot miss something I never knew.

I often tell others that I have been blessed
because I cannot tell most colors apart.
I am not able to judge others by the color of skin
but rather by the content of their heart.

(October 1998)

A PROMISE

How I wish that time had no meaning
but our bodies are cursed by years.
A lifetime would not be long enough
to dry your eyes from one single tear.
A century would be much too short
to tell of the love that I feel for you.
If allowed each second with you in my arms
a thousand years would end much too soon.
Since we know that our time on this earth
will never be enough for you and me...

Each moment I live will be for you
and I will love you for all eternity.

(November 1998)

MOM

You are the one that I call Mom,
I have known you most of my life.
At first, you were an acquaintance,
then you became my father's wife.

At first I really resented you
and purposely got on your nerves.
But you always treated me with kindness
and showed me love that I didn't deserve.

You took the time to teach me things
things like gravity and how to sew.
When I was sick you took care of me
and played with me in the snow.

As I was growing into a man,
you stood behind me in all I tried.
When I succeeded you were behind me,
when I failed you held me while I cried.

I cannot remember when I first called you Mom
or when other's thought of me as your son
But I became the child you could not have
and I feel honored to be that one.

And even though you have loved me so much,
my birth mother you can never be.
But you are the person that I call Mom
And that is all that matters to me.

(December 1998)

FOR YOU

I loved you before we ever met
before your name I ever knew.
Long before I saw your beautiful eyes
my heart belonged to you.

Countless nights have I spent dreaming of you,
what you looked like or the smell of your hair.
But just before seeing you in my mind
I would awake and you would not be there.

At times I doubted if you even existed
or if there was someone out there who...
Could make me love them more each day
and make all of my dreams come true.

In your eyes I see my spirit reborn.
In your kiss my desires are set free.
In your touch I feel my dreams take form.
In your arms my heart finds sanctuary.

(March 2001)

WALKING IN THE RAIN

I often walk out in the rain
alone under the stormy skies.
Where I can spend time by myself
away from other's prying eyes.

Above me the clouds roll like stormy seas
crashing on some unseen shore.
Sending a constant shower of rain
to the earth in a steady downpour.

I treasure my solace during the deluge
when I can navigate through puddles and think.
My thoughts are my only companion
as the world and my spirit drink.

The thunder and the wind stir my soul
forcing the release of my problems and pain.
Where they mix with the water splashing over me
and are washed away by the rain.

Sometimes a rainbow breaks through the clouds
telling me that the storm will soon come to an end.
And there alone for a few precious moments
the world and I feel clean again.

(July 2005)

PROVERBS FOR A DAUGHTER

When I look into your small beautiful eyes
and think of the woman you will grow to be.
I feel lucky to have been given the chance
to hold your hand and see you smile at me.

There are many things I would like to say
if you should ever ask me for advice.
Until that day comes I want to share
some lessons I have learned in my life.

Love God and serve Him with all that you have
and treat your neighbor better than yourself.
Riches and prestige may be important to some
but helping others will bring more valuable wealth.

If you try to accomplish something easy in life
you will usually find that it has already been done.
Set your goals on something that is challenging
and then strive to become number one.

Success is born of preparation, dedication and focus
and your willingness to completely commit.
Compromise any of those and you become average
the worst words you can say is “I quit”.

Cherish the gift that is known as youth
before society tries to tell you who you are.
And listen to the words of those older than you
learn from their wisdom and you will go far.

A few times in life you will be given a chance
to do something that is considered great.
If you put your trust in fate or luck
not being ready will be your biggest mistake.

Your life will be filled with choices and dreams,
you may choose a career, be a wife and a mother.
But the only thing that you will leave on this earth
is how you impact the lives of others.

(August 2005)
~I love you Sweetheart~

THE PATH TO YOU

Throughout my life I have walked
along a path of my own creation.
Decisions I've made have determined my steps
on the road to my life's destination.

Sometimes the path has been straight and true
other times there have been twists and turns.
I have walked over hills and through valleys
and looked back at bridges I have burned.

Occasionally I have stumbled on my path
and at times wandered for a long time lost.
I felt I would continue my path alone
then one day our paths finally crossed.

Now we are walking a path together
where we will face both triumph and trials.
But I look forward to every step with you
and I am thankful for every mile.

The path I walked wasn't always easy
though now I have a new path to share.
I would gladly take each step again
as long as in the end you would be there.

(September 2005)

NOVEMBER 18TH

On a chilly afternoon in November,
three people met under the shade of a tree.
They made a promise to love each other forever,
and then walked away as a family.

(November 2005)

MY REVELATION

A few years ago, I came to a point
where my life no longer made sense.
I was no longer a person I believed in
and my actions offered me no defense.

I found myself looking for answers
in places forgotten or never explored
And soon I began to see my life
with a clarity that I never had before.

I found that the sun will always rise
even when you do not want it to.
No matter how bad things may sometimes be
life will go on with or without you.

I found that pride may go before one's fall
but it sometimes stays with you until the last.
Know that when you look at life's crystal ball
your vision is clearest when you look in the past.

I found that when you are all alone
you can hear the deafening roar of silence.
When trying to solve the problems of life
the best solution is rarely one of violence.

I found that there really is a difference
between a friend and just an acquaintance.
And while waiting for my spirit to heal
the hardest lesson I learned was patience.

Then I found one day that I could smile
when I looked at myself in the mirror.
And I realized that my life had begun to change
when choices once clouded were now clearer.

Others ask if all I went through was worth it
and I always answer them yes because.
By loosing myself and then searching for me
I found out who I truly was.

(January 2006)

PRODIGAL SON

Some people have called me the prodigal son,
a child who wandered far from his home.
Instead of doing what my Father wished of me,
I went out into the world on my own.

The world accepted me with a welcomed change
from the commandments of my Father's kingdom.
Rather than having to obey His unbending rules
I could now concentrate on my new found freedom.

In my new life I was surrounded by many friends
who treated me as if I were a king.
They laughed at my jokes and showed me the world
and let me pay the bills for everything.

The day soon came when my accounts all came due,
and I realized that all my money was gone.
The friends I once had were nowhere to be found
then I had to face my troubles on my own.

A once-loved world now turned its back on me,
I realized that I was penny-less, hungry and alone.
I felt like a prince who had become a pauper
and then a voice deep inside me said, "Go Home."

More than anything I wanted to return home
and walk again through the familiar front door.
Instead of a son I would happily live as a servant
just to be in my Father's home once more.

While I walked the journey to my Father's house
I wondered if He would still call me His son.
Would He forgive me or would He send me away
because my many sins could not be undone?

When I saw my Father running down the road
I feared that pleas for forgiveness would be spurned.
But He said that he'd seen me coming from far away
and He knew that His lost child had finally returned.

I knelt at His feet and begged for His mercy
for the poor choices and mistakes I had made.
Instead He lifted me up gently and held me close
telling me that all of my debts had been paid.

So some people still call me the prodigal son
who left and then returned to his Father's home.
But my journey taught me about a Father's love
that I now share with a child of my own.

(June 2007)

MOON

You are the Earth's constant companion
sharing her travels through space every night.
Giving us company and showing the way,
bathing the land with a pale cloak of white.

You have been worshipped, studied and mapped
by countless cultures throughout the ages.
You are used by man to mark a passage of time
by watching you change with your various stages.

Six times man has walked on your surface
and looked back at the earth from afar.
You allowed us to see a world without borders
helping us to realize how small we really are.

Often I have visited you through a telescope,
traveling in my mind to your sights I can see.
In my dreams I have climbed the rim of Copernicus
and I have sailed across your tranquil sea.

(July 2007)

SHILOH

As a boy I walked the fields of Shiloh
wrapped in the pre-dawn mists by myself all alone.
Following footsteps of men who wore blue and gray
whose many names and faces to history have gone.

I stopped by a cannon on a long forgotten redoubt
standing watch like a sentinel on the crest of hill.
A breeze blew the mist over me like the smoke or war
and across the cannon whose loud roar was now still.

I could almost hear soldier's voices from the past
filling the air with shouts that were long ago cried.
I walked lost until I came upon a military cemetery
I found myself surrounded by those who had died.

The mist faded away as the sun began to shine
and sounds of nature replaced echoes long ceased.
I felt the soldiers and the field where they now lay
had earned the right to rest forever in peace.

(August 2007)

MY DAD

I am the person that you call your son
you've known my name since you were a boy.
We have filled each other's lives with memories
and had our share of both trouble and joy.

Growing up we often struggled in our roles
you tried to teach lessons I did not understand.
The seeds you planted took root and grew with me
producing knowledge I have harvested as a man.

From you I learned my love for history
and my need to question almost everything.
You taught me to honor those who came before us
whose ancient crest we both wear on our rings.

Through my eyes you have explored the world,
fought in war and seen foreign lands.
For years I brought you rocks from my travels
I have put the world piece by piece in your hands.

At times in my life I have been called a hero
a title that I have found difficult to accept as true.
Because when I look back on all of my memories
I know that the real hero in my life was you.

To me you have become more than just my Dad
you are person on whom I trust and depend.
No longer are you just my father;
you are my life-long friend.

(August 2007)

TIME

Time is a gift we start to lose
from the moment that it is given.
And someday I will have to defend
how I spent my time while I was living.

How many days have I spent worrying
about things I could not control?
Instead of trying to change myself
along with the content of my soul.

How many weeks have I spent crying
when faced with sorrow or another's wrath?
Instead of facing the world with a smile
and answering each difficulty with a laugh.

How many months have I spent angry
and holding on to a senseless grudge?
Instead of trying to learn forgiveness
because I too one day will be judged.

How many years have I spent wondering
where all my time has slipped away?
Instead of knowing that I have the chance to change
with the start of each new day.

In the end I guess that time can be
either a blessing or curse.
Invested wisely there is nothing better,
wasted foolishly there is nothing worse.

(September 2007)

OPENING MY WINDOWS

When I was young I suffered a wound in my life
that brought a pain no child should ever know.
As a result I became an emotional invalid
left unable to trust and feeling unwhole.

I spent much of the first year in a day dream
drawing pictures of castles as a way to cope.
I decided to close all the windows to my soul
from a world where I could not find any hope.

As I grew I learned to hide my fears deep inside
keeping everyone who met me at arm's length.
I deceived the world from all of my hidden pain
camouflaging me became my greatest strength.

Looking at myself I saw only damaged goods
I felt as if I were broken and now bore a stain.
Often I would sabotage my own relationships
so that I could regulate the extent of my pain.

One day I understood that I had become a slave
to memories of events that occurred long ago.
Instead of protecting I was only hurting myself
by letting the pain of my past be in control.

Then I realized that letting others inside
was the only way that I could be free.
So I opened all the windows to my soul
for all of the world to see.

(February 2008)

About the Author

William Eric Stevens was born and grew up in Hot Springs, Arkansas. He is a veteran of the Arkansas Army National Guard and the United States Air Force. An avid history buff, William has been fascinated with the Civil War since his childhood.

William has enjoyed writing stories and poems for as long as he can remember, but began to write the poetry contained in this book in 1996. In 2008 he earned a Professional in Human Resources (PHR) certification. He lives in Little Rock, Arkansas with his wife, Juliet and daughter, Mackynzie. This is his first book.

You can contact Will at:

opening_my_windows@hotmail.com

www.ingramcontent.com/pod-product-compliance
Ingram Content Group UK Ltd.
Pitfield, Milton Keynes, MK11 3LW, UK
UKHW041925190726
13854UKWH00003B/1453

9 780557 515165